The Six O'clock in the Morning, Worth Getting Up For, Only Seven Minutes, Kids of All Ages, Fun Breakfasts Cookbook

by Chef Pierre Ange A.K.A. Peter H. Engel

The Six O'clock in the Morning, Worth Getting Up For, Only Seven Minutes, Kids of All Ages, Fun Breakfasts Cookbook

by Chef Pierre Ange A.K.A. Peter H. Engel

Project Editor: Lisa M. Tooker
Illustrations: Mathieu Gibault
Design and Production: Christine Gross

Printed in Korea

ISBN: 978-1-59637-116-3

Contents

Yonder see the morning glint

The sun is up, and up must I

To wash and dress, and eat and drink

And look at things, and talk and think

And work.

And God knows why!

WAKE UP, KIDS!

Have you ever tried to get your children out of bed on a school day? Not easy! (At my house we occasionally drizzle cold water on their heads; you do that once a year and the threat will last about twelve months before you have to repeat the actual act. In between, an empty beaker and a loaded threat does the trick.)

More seriously, once they are up, there's the question of what to prepare for breakfast. You want to send them off with a nutritious, tasty, hot meal. Don't you? How else are they going to pass today's spelling test? And if they fail that, will they ever get into medical school? I doubt it. However, important though nutrition is, at that time of the morning, you certainly don't want to have to work at it. And, if you're like me, you're not in a very good position to think.

In any case, by the time you finally persuade the kids to stagger to the table (with or without the water torture), they're already late. There's no time for a lot of cooking.

"I'm not hungry."

"Eggs again, yuk!"

"Why do we always have to have a cooked breakfast?"

"I want a Pop Tart."

"I'm tired (pronounced 'ti-i-ired')."

It's the inevitable litany. Perish the thought that any kid worth his or her salt would ever say something as outrageous as, "Thanks for cooking me a great breakfast."

So what's the answer?

Simple! I found it. Cook something the kids will enjoy. Something that takes no more than, say, seven minutes to prepare. Be creative. Make breakfast fun.

You have to be kidding. At six o'clock in the morning? Be creative? Have fun?

Yep! And this is the book that will show you how. From now on, you can make some-thing different *every day for weeks*. And everything you make will be nutritionally sound; appealing to kids of all ages, in fact, so appealing that they'll actually feel breakfast is worth getting up for; and so easy to make that even a near-comatose, non-chef like me (and most crack-of-dawn parents of my acquaintance) can prepare it in seven minutes or less.

EASY NUTRITION

I am not about to give you a lecture on healthy eating or dieting. If you are over-weight, eat less. If you're fat, eat a lot less. Those are the only diets that are guaran-teed to work.

They say that diets don't work. "They," as usual, are wrong. Of course diets work. I have lost the same 10 pounds at least 50 times in my life. If I hadn't gone on a diet to lose those familiar 10 pounds every time I regained them, I would weigh 500 pounds more than I do.

Exercise helps, too. However, since this is a book about breakfast, and six-o'clock-in-the-morning breakfast at that, exercise is irrelevant. No one I know – or care to know – exercises at that time of the morning.

However, nutrition is important, and the fact is that most breakfast foods are, to put it mildly, nutritionally challenged. Cereals, including hot cereals such as oatmeal, grits, etc., contain mostly carbohydrates, those famous "empty calories." Eggs are full of protein, but also full of cholesterol and fat. Bacon is even worse because, in addition to its protein, it contains lots of fat and an excessive amount of salt. Fruit would be a good thing to serve at breakfast, but I have found that most people don't bother. And as for vegetables, nobody serves them for breakfast.

Fortunately, help is at hand. Every recipe in this book (well, nearly every recipe) contains at least some protein, limited fat, and even less saturated fat (the really nasty kind). And most of the recipes include some fruit or veggies.

Of course, some recipes are better for you than others. And, by the famous Law of Natural Cussedness, the least nutritionally sound tend to be the ones the kids like the best. So I suggest you mix 'em up a bit. Serve the ones that contain relatively high amounts of saturated fat and cholesterol (whole eggs, butter, etc.) only at most two times a week. The rest of the time, serve breakfast foods that have protein with little or no cholesterol.

TRICKS OF THE TRADE

A word about eggs

Egg whites are almost pure protein, contain virtually no fat, and are almost tasteless. They mix readily with almost anything. Thus, they are a perfect addition to any food (such as oatmeal, for example) that, without help, has little to offer nutritionally.

You could also add a whole egg. However, while you'd be adding more protein (since there is about the same amount of protein in the average egg yoke as in the average egg white), you'd also be adding lots of fat and cholesterol. When you are making something in which you can "hide" some egg whites, it is probably a good idea to do so. Even when you are making scrambled eggs or an egg omelet, I would suggest that you use half whole eggs and half egg whites. Of course, you could use only egg whites and make a perfectly formed omelet out of them. However, they would not have much taste to them. I don't recommend egg white omelets, at least not for kids.

What you do with the egg yokes when you separate them out is up to you. For example, you could make Hollandaise sauce with them. Or, you could throw them out. I generally store them for a while and then throw them out.

What's in a name?

The thing about kids is they're gullible. When it comes to food, unless it's spinach or something adults only can be convinced to eat, kids can be talked into liking almost anything, even stuff that kids generally hate (which is anything they perceive might possibly be good for them). So the trick is to add some glamour to whatever you're making for breakfast.

There are four basic ways of adding glamour. (You may think there are more than four, but you'll soon see that all the techniques you can think of boil down to four.)

Glam Names

You must admit that Cheese Eggs Grande Luxe sounds better than "scrambled eggs with cheese and bacon." And that Froatmeal beats out "oatmeal with fruit."

When you're trying to convince kids to eat breakfast, always grace your latest creation with a glamorous name. And, the more mundane the food, the more high-fallutin' the name.

The fact is, if the food you've prepared (slightly burnt, perhaps, or otherwise barely edible) has a good name, you'll probably end up convincing the kids that they love it.

Introducing the Chef

My name, as you might have noticed in glancing at the cover of the book, is Peter Engel. That surname means angel in German. The French for angel is ange. The French, by and large, prepare wonderful food, although nowadays they eat at MacDonald's with increasing – and alarming – frequency, which is less wonderful. Therefore, cleverly putting two and two together, to give my morning creations a little cachet, I have invented that culinary superstar, Chef Pierre Ange.

Of course, my kids don't believe there really is such a Chef. They're almost seven years old and worldly wise beyond belief. But it's fun to go along with Dad's silly game. Like the tooth fairy, Santa Claus, and the Easter Bunny, Chef Pierre Ange brings them things they like – so why not go along with the gag? Anyhow, he might, just might, really exist.

Famous Endorsements

Of course, endorsements don't end with the putative chef. They can be expanded to include anyone who, no doubt, would love these recipes if only they had the chance to try them. For example, Julia Roberts, through her fan club, once stated categorically (in response to a question from the Food Maestro himself) that she wished Chef Pierre Ange good luck in his endeavors. A huge endorsement, right? Indeed, when asked more directly about him, she is rumored to have said, "Huh?" Well, there you have it!

Similar comments have been heard from various other celebrities. In fact the last two Presidents of the United States – yes, Bill and Dubya – both refrained from inviting Chef Pierre to the White House even once, realizing, no doubt, that he would be far too busy to accept such an interruption of his breakfast duties.

Forbidden Food

Some foods, as every parent knows, are simply not allowed. No, Johnny, you can't have jam on your scrambled eggs. No Susie, marshmallows are not appropriate for toast. Yes, darling, I know you like fish fingers, chicken tenders, macaroni-and-cheese, hamburgers, and ketchup...but they're not for breakfast.

The thing is, why not?

Breaking the rules from time to time – and swearing the kids to secrecy ("don't let Mommy find out") – adds excitement to the breakfast table. Of course, you can't do it too often otherwise the thrill evaporates. Anyway, why not have jam on scrambled eggs? Omelets made with jam are a popular French dish. The Japanese eat raw fish and pickled vegetables for breakfast. The English (for some unknown reason) eat kippers, an exceedingly salty, smoked herring with more bones than any known creature. So what's wrong with having last night's macaroni and cheese? Heat it up, pop a strawberry on top of the pile on each plate (to show how really wicked you are), call it Morning Macaroni, and watch them wolf down a good, nutritious, hot breakfast.

Of course, you usually don't have leftovers left over. Or if you do, it's because the kids wouldn't eat their supper. No amount of camouflage will resuscitate that sort of left over.

"Daaa-ad. Not THAT again..."

Pride of Chefmanship

Even young kids can crack eggs into a bowl. Or stir up scrambled eggs and cheese. Moreover, when it comes to exotic mixtures, no one is more creative than 12-year-olds egged on by their younger siblings. As long as you keep the breakfast simple, kids can help. And they will always eat with more enthusiasm something they have prepared – or helped prepare – than something placed in front of them.

We have a rule in my house: You have the right to put anything (reasonable) you want onto the table. But if it's not on the table by the time we all sit down to eat, you're out of luck. ("Reasonable" is in the eye of the beholder. And the beholder is me! Whoever said that parenting was a democratic process?) Giving kids this sort of authority works pretty well. The kids set the table most days. Of course, they do tend to forget napkins.

There you are, four ways to get the kids interested in the seven-minute breakfast you are about to prepare. Easy. Even early in the morning. So, let's get on with it by starting with the eggs…

EGGS

Fried Eggs

We'll start with something deceptively simple – which, as every non-chef knows, is not simple at all, fried eggs. The problem with fried eggs is they either crack when you drop them into the pan or break when you try to flip them over. To avoid them breaking, *The Joy of Cooking*, the grandmamma of all cookbooks, recommends "when the whites are firm, insert a slotted spatula under the egg," (now where could that slotted spatula have gone to?)

"supporting the yoke area, and cautiously reverse it in the skillet." Yeah, right! At 6:30 a.m., of course they'll break!

You could eat them "sunny side up," of course. Then you wouldn't have to flip them. But if you do that, they'll either be leathery on the bottom, or too runny on the top (and, in my book, under-cooked egg whites score high on kids' "gross out" list).

$\rightarrow$ So here's what you do:
Have you noticed that, when you intend to make scrambled eggs, the yolks almost never break when you drop them into the pan? That's because you are being casual about it, and not thinking about how to break the shells. When you think about it, you either crack them too hard and break the yoke; or not hard enough so that you have to hit them again or pry them apart – and break the yoke.

So from now on, pretend you're making scrambled eggs when you're actually planning to fry them.

Never decide whether you're making scrambled eggs or fried eggs until they're all in the pan! If they break, you were planning on scrambled; if they don't, fried was your plan. By following this simple rule, you will never again break an egg you were intending to fry unbroken.

Once the eggs are in the pan unbroken, instead of flipping them, or trying to achieve the perfect sunny side up, cover the frying eggs with a saucepan lid. (This has the added advantage that it avoids grease spatters around the stove. Of course, you do have an extra lid to clean. But that will go into the dishwasher with no problem.) Choose a lid that is rounded enough so its top doesn't touch the eggs. Under the lid, they'll cook in no time*. When you remove the lid, sometimes they'll look like ordinary sunny side up eggs, sometimes like a cross between "over easy" and "sunny side up." I've no idea why this varies; it just does. But in either case, no leathery bottom; no breakage; no problem.

If you don't have one already, buy yourself a Teflon-coated frying pan. And whenever you're frying something, put a little olive oil onto the pan to add to its non-stick surface. By the way, the most convenient way of doing this is to buy a can of Pam and spritz it over the pan's surface. Pam is just olive oil in an aerosol can. If you do this while the pan is over a flame, you will have a pretty good chance of causing a flame thrower effect. Provided you remain suitably insouciant as you singe your eyebrows, this will impress the kids. (However, please be careful and turn off the gas before you do the spritzing.) With this pan and the oil, you will never have trouble getting the eggs out of the pan. They'll slip right onto the plate. Delicious.

Of course, frying eggs means that you cannot eliminate any of the yolks so you always get a full dose of the eggs' cholesterol together with their protein. (With scrambled eggs, you can mix half full eggs with half egg whites. The kids won't notice the difference.) Don't worry – you won't be eating fried eggs that often!

Now that you have the basic principle of frying (or scrambling) eggs, you have just opened the door to any number of delicious alternatives. Remember, there is nothing you can make with fried eggs that you cannot also make with scrambled eggs. In fact, some non-chefs have given up on frying eggs altogether, and only scramble them. However, since I am a purist, I recommend you choose fried eggs whenever they happen to come out like they should.

*Well, actually, about two minutes, but it depends on the heat, the thickness of the pan, and a few other imponderables, so you'll have to peek the first time you do this.

Bacon and Eggs

There are two ways of preparing bacon. One way is easy: you put rashers of bacon (layered between paper towels to catch the spatter) into the microwave. Two or three minutes later (depending on how powerful your microwave is) you have reasonably crisp, reasonably bland bacon.

The other way is to fry the bacon. That way it's super crisp and super delicious. The trouble is, frying bacon is a pain. It spatters; it smells up the whole house; and, unless you watch carefully, the bacon will end up either undercooked and floppy-greasy, or overcooked and burnt tasting. On the other hand, bacon, when it comes out right, is very good indeed.

Now that you've learned how to make fried eggs without ever breaking them, let me explain what to do to achieve perfectly fried bacon.

There's no getting away from frying bacon once. However, there is no need to keep repeating the chore every time you want to use some. Instead, set aside a day (preferably a miserable, rainy day when you have something boring to do in the afternoon, so that it's a wasted day anyhow), and cook up several batches – as much bacon as you expect to use, let's say, for three months. Longer, if you do not make bacon that often at home.

I use two pans. But don't empty out the fat between batches. Bacon cooks much more evenly when there's a lot of fat in the pan – it deep fries the bacon. Watch the bacon carefully as it cooks so that you don't burn it.

Remove each batch from the heat when nicely crisp. As you take each rasher out, lay it flat on some paper towels, and blot the top with more towels to get rid of as much grease as possible.

Now place the degreased bacon into several plastic baggies. Keep one baggie in the refrigerator for use in the next week or two, and freeze the rest.

The preparation time will take more than seven minutes, however, after the first time, it won't take more than a few seconds.

When you get ready to make a breakfast with bacon, all you need to do is to take out the amount you need and cook it just long enough to get it warm, probably no more than 30 seconds in the hot pan in which you fried the eggs. Almost no muss or fuss, and Voila: crisp bacon! (You could also warm up the pan-fried bacon in the microwave. But in my experience, it comes out limp. Maybe the difference has to do with the time of day; nothing seems particularly crisp at 6:00 a.m.)

Ange McMuffin

My apologies to Mickey D's for the name, but this one is better anyhow. A gourmet repast that takes five minutes tops!

Serves 1

> ½ **English muffin**
> 2 **slices American cheese**
> 2 **slices bacon (or other meat), cooked**
> 1 **Fried Egg (see recipe on page 18)**

Toast half of an English muffin until lightly toasted. Layer one slice of American cheese, bacon or some other cooked meat, and fried egg (that, in this case, you have slightly undercooked which, by the way, has saved you a little time) on top of muffin. Place second slice of cheese on top of egg.

Heat in the microwave until the top slice of cheese starts to melt, probably about 10 to 20 seconds.

Ange McSalmon

Use the same ingredients and recipe instructions as the Ange McMuffin, but use smoked salmon instead of the bacon or meat. If you're a purist, forget the cheese and add a little more salmon.

I warn you, however, most kids don't like smoked salmon. But some do…and those that do love this variation. So, as they say with cleaning fluids, check out a little bit of the salmon on a kid before committing yourself to the whole thing.

Serves 1

> ½ **English muffin**
> 2 **slices American cheese**
> 2 **slices smoked salmon**
> 1 **Fried Egg (see recipe on page 18)**

Egg en Troue

This is French for egg in a hole.
It sounds better in French!

Serves 1–2

> **2 slices soft white bread
> (e.g., Wonder bread)**
> **2 eggs**
> **Honey**

Take two slices of soft bread and place them on top of each other on a hard surface. Take a glass with a diameter that is slightly smaller than the bread slices and use the glass to punch out a hole in the center of the bread.

If you have used soft bread, you'll be left with two slices of bread each with a nice round hole, and a round, fat little "pillow" of two pieces of bread, the cutouts from the holes, stuck together. Reserve the pillows or bread pieces for later use.

Place the bread slices with the holes into a frying pan and break in one egg into each hole. If it happens to break, stir it up so that it looks scrambled, as if you did it on purpose. Now fry the egg with the lid on the whole thing. In this case, you can afford to overcook the egg somewhat. That way, the kids can eat it by hand, without having to cut it up.

If you prefer, you can flip the whole bread-egg. The egg is unlikely to break because it's held in place by the bread.

While you're waiting for the eggs to finish cooking, put the pillows of bread or bread pieces in the pan and brown on both sides. Then add a dollop of honey on top: the perfect side dish with the eggs. Well, it is for kids. (The only problem is that you may want to serve only one egg per child. In that case, you will only have one pillow so plan accordingly.)

> **Note:**
> *If you have a cookie-cutter of the right size, you can use it to make a fun shape in the center instead of a round hole. However, because cookie-cutters are sharp, the slices of bread don't always stick together.*

Eggs In Hiding

The name alone makes this a favorite with kids.

Serves 1–2

> **2 slices soft white bread
> (e.g., Wonder bread)
> 2 eggs
> 1 slice meat, cheese, or tomato
> (or combination of all)**

Use the same recipe and ingredients as Eggs en Troue (on page 24), but before the eggs are done, cover the bread-egg with a layer of camouflage like meat, cheese or tomato slices, or all of the above. Continue to heat the combination under the saucepan lid until everything is nice and warm. If you use cheese, the top layer should be just starting to melt.

Scrambled Eggs

Scrambled eggs are the easiest, quickest, and most versatile for breakfast. To start, you can make a scrambled egg version of anything you can make with fried eggs. (Remember, unless they happened to end up fried, you *intended* to make them scrambled!)

You can add almost any type of leftover you have in the refrigerator to scrambled eggs – and something the kids don't object to.

Leftovers that taste great with scrambled eggs, and that, in some form or another, you will be more likely to find in your refrigerator, include: all forms of meat (if it's tough or hard, you'll have to grind it up); and every known type of cooked vegetable. Raw veggies are as good – often even better – if they're the type that people like to eat raw.

Because you can make so many different dishes with scrambled eggs, I'm only going to list a few here. However, whenever you add something new to the eggs, something you've never had around before, roast ostrich perhaps, remember to give the dish a new, exotic name. (Aussie Eggs might work.)

Before we go any further, let's make sure you know how to make perfect scrambled eggs.

egg in hiding

Perfect Scramblers

Of course, you know how to make scrambled eggs. They are nothing more than a few eggs cracked into a frying pan and stirred while heating. However, to make *perfect* scrambled eggs, here are four tips:

→ As mentioned earlier, to reduce the amount of cholesterol per serving, make your scrambled eggs with a mixture of whole eggs and egg whites. About 50/50 is what the Chef recommends.

→ Add just a little bit of milk (or even half and half) to your eggs. About 1 tablespoon per egg. It will make your scramblers taste much creamier.

→ Instead of adding salt to the eggs, cook them salt-free. Then put some large-grain sea salt on the table and let eaters drop a few grains onto their eggs. The piquant contrast between no salt eggs and salty "points of flavor" improves the whole dish.

→ Some people like their scrambled eggs as soft as thick cream; some like them medium; some like them so hard they practically bounce off the plate. Therefore, it's wise to ask people how they like them. It's easy to accommodate everyone by taking portions for the "softies" off first, and cooking the "toughies" a little longer. However, remember that the eggs keep on hardening up after you remove them from the pan so take them out of the pan just before they reach their desired hardness.

Here are some of my favorite scrambled egg dishes.

Cheese Eggs (de Luxe)

The difference between ordinary cheese eggs and the deluxe version is in the amount of cheese you use. The ordinary version uses one slice of American cheese (or the equivalent in other cheeses) for two eggs. The deluxe version doubles the amount of cheese. If you're a cheese person, you'll prefer the deluxe. If you're not, I'd steer clear of cheese eggs altogether. So, as far as I am concerned, it's Cheese Eggs *de Luxe* or nothing.

You can use many kinds of cheese in eggs: American, cheddar, Gouda, Jack, etc. However, I'd stay away from the really "stinky" cheeses. They overpower the egg taste.

Serves 1–2

**1 slice American cheese
(or cheddar, Gouda or Jack)
2 eggs (if desired, use half white
and half yolk)
2 tablespoons milk (or half and half)
Sea salt (optional)**

Cheese Eggs Grande Luxe

I realize this is gilding the lily. But…if you really want something out of this world, take out one of your baggies of bacon, crisp it up (very crisp) by pan frying a little longer than usual, and then crumble the bacon into the Cheese Eggs *de Luxe* mix.

Serves 1–2

**1 slice American cheese
(or cheddar, Gouda or Jack)
2 eggs
2 tablespoons milk (or half and half)
Bacon, cooked and crumbled
Sea salt (optional)**

Yogurt Scramblers

Forget the milk in your scrambled eggs, and add cup plain yogurt for every two eggs. To spice this up, you may want to add one tablespoon per two eggs of any of the following: ketchup, barbecue sauce, or soy sauce. If you use barbecue sauce, make sure it's not the sweet kind. That sort tastes fine with spare ribs, but with eggs it tastes evil.

Alternatively, instead of yogurt alone, you can use a 50/50 mixture of yogurt and mayonnaise. You can also add Lawry's Season Salt to taste.

- **2 eggs**
- **¼ cup plain yogurt**
- **1 tablespoon ketchup,**
  or barbecue or soy sauce
- **Sea salt or Lawry's Season Salt (optional)**

Fresh Veggie Scramblers

This may be my favorite scrambled egg dish. And it's ridiculously easy! All you do is to scramble your eggs in the normal manner, and a few moments before you are ready to take them off the heat, stir in some fresh cut vegetables.

Serves 1–2

- **2 eggs**
- **2 tablespoons milk (or half and half)**
- **¼ cup diced fresh raw vegetables**
  (e.g., tomatoes, mushrooms, peas,
  avocado, carrots, celery, artichoke
  hearts)
- **Sea salt (optional)**

Add diced tomatoes, raw mushrooms, fresh peas, chunks of avocado; shredded carrots; finely diced celery, artichoke hearts; shelled edamame; diced olives, capers (okay, I know, technically those aren't uncooked); and any other vegetables you like to eat raw. (I like diced uncooked cauliflower.)

The nice part about this is that you get the advantages of both a hot breakfast, and the benefits of fresh veggies (which every health expert agrees are essential for your kids' well-being). And even kids who normally don't like vegetables like them in this form.

Veggie Scramblers Normale

This works the same as the fresh vegetable version, except you use leftover cooked vegetables. Yep, it's more plebian than the fresh version. That's why it has to have a French name. Still, it's an excellent way to use up yesterday's uneaten whatever. The only thing you have to watch out for is that, if the vegetables are soggy, don't add any milk to the scrambled eggs.

Serves 1–2

2 eggs
2 tablespoons milk (or half and half)
¼ cup cooked vegetables
Sea salt (optional)

Framblers

Framblers are made the same as Fresh Veggie Scramblers, but using fruit instead of vegetables. Diced apples, pears, strawberries, raspberries, bananas, peaches, apricots (if you like them which I don't), seedless grapes, or any mixture tastes delicious. Citrus fruits don't, and I've never tried melons because I don't like them hot. Remember, dice the fruit you choose finely. If you leave biggish chunks, some kids will pick out the fruit and leave the eggs. Little monsters! For added crunch (and protein), add some peanuts.

Most kids like framblers with brown sugar. Some people say you have to be a kid to appreciate that. But I like it just as much as my boys. And why not? As long as they don't take too much, I let them have it. Heck, it's 6.30 a.m., not the time to argue.

Serves 1–2

2 eggs
2 tablespoons milk (or half and half)
¼ cup diced fresh fruit (e.g., apples, pears, strawberries, raspberries, bananas, peaches, apricots, grapes)
Peanuts (optional)
Brown sugar (optional)
Sea salt (optional)

Poached Eggs

Poached eggs have the advantage of not being greasy. They have the disadvantage, as with fried eggs, that you cannot eliminate any of the yolks. Still, unless you or your kids are getting too much fat in your diets – for example, if you are visiting McDonald's more than about once a year – poached eggs are a good alternative to either fried or scrambled.

However, the only way to make poached eggs is to buy some individual poaching molds. Lightly oil up the molds with a small amount of olive oil. Break one egg into each mold. Place the molds in a frying pan with about half an inch of water. (If you break any of the eggs, get rid of the water, dump the whole thing into the frying pan, add some egg whites, and revert to scramblers.) Bring the water to a boil and place a lid over the pan. Check the hardness of the eggs by touching them with a handy spoon or other implement. They should be soft, but not runny. Turn the mold over onto a plate and, if the eggs don't come out, tap the bottom of the mold.

If they still won't come out, turn them right side up again, and run a knife around the edge of the mold. When you turn them this time, chances are they will pop out and try to skid onto the floor. So be warned.

Here are some of the more interesting things you can make with poached eggs.

Apple Poachers

This is a very unusual dish. No one but Chef Pierre Ange would have dared to be this innovative. But, against the odds, it actually tastes delectable – and, if you serve it with aplomb, the kids won't realize how odd their parent is until it's too late and they're already enjoying what they're eating. As with all my breakfast dishes, this one is very easy to prepare.

Poach an egg and toast half an English muffin. Those are your raw materials.

Take an apple with about the same diameter as the muffin, and cut a slice from its widest point. Cut out the core from the center of the slice. Now you have an apple ring. Put the ring on top of the muffin, and the poached egg on top of the ring. Voila!

If your apple isn't big enough to form a ring, place two slices (half moons) onto the muffin with a gap between before you place the poached egg on top.

Why the ring or the half circles of apple, you may ask? Because if you put a whole slice of apple onto the muffin, when you try to balance the egg on top, it will usually slip off, quite probably onto the floor where it will break and the kids will step in it...and on top of that calamity, they will (inevitably) say:

"Apples and eggs... Yuck! Daaa-ad!"

Sticky Poachers

Serves 1

) 1 egg
1 slice English muffin
1 slice American cheese
Egg mold
Olive oil for mold

Poach one or more eggs, a little softer than usual (but not so soft that they go splat when you tip them out of their molds); and toast as many muffin slices as you have eggs. Place one poached egg on each muffin slice. Cover with one or two slices of American cheese. Pop them into the microwave until cheese melts...maybe 10 or 15 seconds.

That's it. They're called sticky because, when the kids go to cut them, the melted cheese will stick to the knife. There is no way around this. So, make sure the knives are blunt and turn a blind eye when the kids eat the cheese off the knife. Breaking rules is such fun!

By the way, here's a tip if you have younger kids. Precut the toasted English muffin into bite-sized pieces before putting the egg on top. That way when they go to cut the egg it's an easy task.

Eggs Benedict

This is the most famous poached egg breakfast, really the traditional dish made with poached eggs. This is not a kids' meal at all. However, it's a very sophisticated dish and I imagine you may find uses for it. It's also very easy to make.

You can make eggs Benedict either with bacon, Canadian bacon, ham, or smoked salmon. Personally, I don't like Canadian bacon. (When you make Eggs Benedict with salmon, it's called Eggs Benedict with Salmon.) Some people, probably living in California, claim that you can make eggs Benedict with avocado instead of meat. No way, man!

Here's how you make them…

Serves 1

- **1 slice English muffin**
- **2 slices meat or fish (e.g., Canadian bacon, bacon, smoked salmon)**
- **1 egg, poached**
- **Hollandaise sauce**

Toast one half of an English muffin; when lightly toasted, place one slice of the meat/fish you choose onto the muffin; then place the poached egg on top; and layer on a second slice of meat/fish.

Once you're ready to start eating, pour on some Hollandaise sauce. (You want to do this at the last moment to avoid the muffin getting soggy.)

I could tell you how to make the hollandaise. But it's a tedious job involving lots of egg yokes, squeezed lemons, drizzling in melted butter, and beating. One time in two the whole thing curdles and you have to start again. So it's easier to buy the hollandaise at your local supermarket.

Although there is some debate about the matter, the consensus is that the dish is named after Lemuel Benedict, a then important – and swinging – Wall Street broker. Sometime in 1894, he was eating at the still famous and glamorous Waldorf Astoria Hotel in New York, suffering from a debilitating, carousal-induced hangover. He asked Oscar Tschirky, the Waldorf's legendary chef, for a cure, groaning that a poached egg might help. And the rest is history. (Much later, Delmonico's restaurant in New York got in on the act and claimed that they had invented the dish.)

Since you probably won't be having the Eggs Benedict until the kids are safely off to school, you might as well combine it with a mimosa (champagne and fresh orange juice) and enjoy the morning.

Boiled Eggs

Boiled eggs are just about the easiest thing to cook since they involve nothing but boiling water. Unfortunately, as a breakfast food, they are also boring (known to kids as boor-ING).

There is also the problem that it is hard to get them to the right hardness. That is because there are so many variations which effect cooking time: the size of the eggs, their degree of coldness out of the refrigerator, their age, and even the altitude. (As you no doubt remember from your school days, water boils at a lower temperature at higher altitudes than at sea level.)

However, most cooking problems have solutions. Here are two ways to avoid fussing with how hard your boiled eggs are, and at the same time making them into a favorite breakfast dish.

Butter-speared Eggs

This is not a particularly healthy breakfast, but it's okay once in a while. Also, at least for younger kids, it's a bit messy as the egg shells tend to crack, and bits of egg end up on the floor. On the other hand, as breakfasts go, this one is high on the list of improving young kids' fine motor skills...which is what kindergarten and first grade are all about. So you can console yourself that this is an educational breakfast.

Serves 1

1 egg
Butter

Boil the eggs for about seven minutes, or until they are hard or almost hard. Serve them in an egg cup. (We don't have any egg cups in our house, so we use small sake or liqueur glasses.) Remember to put the blunter end of the egg at the top; that's where there is a small air pocket and a thicker layer of egg white, so that it is easier to de-cap. Slice off the tops of the eggs with the sharp blow of a blunt knife.

Now, take a rectangle of butter from the refrigerator, slice off one corner into a "spear," and push it down into the egg. The egg will try to push the butter back up, but after a brief struggle, the butter will melt and a rather dry boiled egg will turn into a buttery delight.

Daddy Eggs

These were named by my sons when they were four years old because only Daddy made eggs like this. They are a variation on scrambled eggs, but many people think they taste better.

Serves 2

5 eggs
Olive oil

For two servings, boil five eggs for five minutes. Take out one, but leave the rest still boiling. Remove the shell and drop it into a bowl. It will still be fairly soft. Now take out the next egg, which will be a little harder and, removing its shell in turn, add it to the first egg. Do the same with the remaining three eggs. Now in your bowl you have all five eggs, including one softish, one a little hard, one medium hard, and two very hard. Remove the yolks of the two hardest eggs, and feed them to the dog. With a fork, mash up the rest. You will find that, combined, they have just the right mixture of "squishiness."

If you want to serve only one person and need only two eggs, let them both get hard. In that case, or if you have let your five eggs get too hard, just add a little olive oil when you mash up the eggs.

In either case, there you have it: a unique form of scrambled eggs.

Eier-im-Glass

(The word "Eier" is pronounced I-er)

This is a traditional German breakfast dish. At least, that's what my Father, who loved them, assured me. Why would I doubt him? Again, it's at the low end of sound nutrition (what traditional German cooking isn't?) so serve only occasionally.

Serves 1–2

2 eggs, hard-boiled
Butter, salted
Toast, sliced

All you do is put two nearly hard-boiled, de-shelled eggs (or three eggs if you're really hungry) into a glass, add a lump of salty butter, and break them up with a spoon. Then eat them out of the glass with a side of toast.

My kids love Eier-im-Glass because it's fun to smash them in the glass. The eggs make pleasantly disgusting squishy sounds. And if they are not quite hard, they squirt funny yolk patterns onto the side of the glass. But beware: if the eggs are even softer, the yolk patterns are liable to cover a somewhat wider arc.

For reasons that I fail to understand, even though they have the same ingredients, Eier-im-Glass taste different than all the other forms of boiled eggs mentioned. The power of suggestion? Try it, you'll see.

OMELETTES

Please note the spelling of this word. According to the dictionary, the more common spelling is "Omelet." However, that would be thoroughly mundane, way beneath the dignity of Chef Pierre Ange who never makes anything "common."

The thing about omelettes is that most people, especially "breakfast only" cooks like me, think making them is difficult and time-consuming. That's certainly what I thought before I tried it the first time: so French, so tricky. Not at all. The truth is you can make an omelette in no more than five minutes. And it's as easy as pie. Magnifique! (Actually it's infinitely easier than pie, a dish I would not even try to make, at least not for breakfast.)

Serves 1–2

> **2-3 eggs**
> **Pinch baking soda (optional)**
> **Cooking spray or olive oil**

Crack two or three eggs per omelette, depending on how hungry your brood is. Mix 'em around a bit in a bowl.

If you like your omelettes "fluffy," which personally I don't, you can beat the eggs into a bit of a froth. If you really want them super fluffy, you can do one of two things:

→ Separate the eggs from the yolks. Throw out some of the yolks. Beat the egg whites until they are stiff enough to stand up in little peaks when you pull out your beater. Then mix the beaten whites back into the remaining yolks.

→ Alternatively, after removing some of the yolks, but without separating the rest of the whites and yolks, add a little baking soda and beat the mixture with extra determination.

Either way, the omelettes will look luscious. However, I find that frothing them up blands down their taste. It's also more work than I care to do, especially in the morning.

Spritz a frying pan with Pam, or oil it up with a teaspoon of olive oil. Heat the frying pan. (It's hot enough if, when you drop a bead of water onto it, the bead jumps around like a flea in a fit, making a snake-like hiss.) Pour the eggs, frothy or not, as you prefer, into the pan. Now tip the pan side to side so that the eggs spread out to cover the surface in a nice, even layer.

Omelettes harden up very quickly. Therefore, after just a few seconds, that is before the top of the eggs hardens, remove the pan from the heat. Now put whatever you want into the center of the eggs (we'll get to what that might be in a moment). If the filling is very cold, you may want to warm it up before adding it to the omelette.

Get hold of each side of the thin egg "pancake" with a fork, and fold the edges over the middle. It's much easier to fold in the two sides than to try for a single fold omelette, and it actually looks more elegant. Put the pan back onto the heat just long enough for the filling to get warm and the eggs to finish setting up. Slide the finished omelette out of the pan onto a plate. (If you have several omelettes to make, put the finished ones into a warm, not hot, oven. You don't want them to get cold; you also don't want them to keep on cooking. But try not to keep them too long, since omelettes – like many of us – tend to toughen up if they are kept waiting.) Serve, and step back to admire your handiwork.

Fillings

Almost any left over makes a good filling for an omelette. Because eggs are so bland, they will go well with nearly everything. Just remember not to put anything into the center of the omelette that is larger than bite size (or that will not melt in the limited amount of heat you can apply to the inside of the omelette). For example, if you want to add meat, sausage, etc., to your omelette, make sure you cut it into small pieces.

Cheese Omelette

Most cheeses will do. But kids generally prefer slices of American cheese. It also has the advantage of melting at exactly the temperature you want on the inside of an omelette. If you don't like that sort of cheese, choose any you do like. But you probably want to avoid the harsher (smellier) varieties. If you choose a hard, slow melting cheese such as cheddar, cut it into small pieces and add it as soon as you have the eggs in the pan.

Always remember to add plenty of cheese. No one likes a cheese omelette where you have to search for the cheese.

Serves 1–2

2–3 eggs
Pinch baking soda (optional)
Cooking spray or olive oil
1–3 slices American cheese
  (or your favorite cheese)

Omelette Fines Herbes

The real version of this omelette has "fine herbs" added to the eggs before they are put into the pan. These herbs usually consist of: parsley, chives, and chervil. Even if you happen to have parsley and chives on hand (a possibility because they both come in a dried form available at your local supermarket), you are obviously unlikely to be able to lay your hands on chervil at this time of the morning – or, for that matter, at any other time of the day. So my version of this excellent omelette is simpler.

Serves 1–2

2–3 eggs
Pinch baking soda (optional)
Cooking spray or olive oil
1–3 slices American cheese
  (or your favorite cheese)
Fresh herbs or dried
  (e.g., parsley, chives, and/or chervil)
Fresh vegetables, cooked and diced

Prepare omelette as in the Omelettes recipe (on page 44). If you happen to have any fresh herbs, by all means add them. If you want to use the dried versions, you'll have to soften them up in a little hot water or milk before adding them to the omelette. Personally, I wouldn't bother. In the center of the omelette, add any leftover cooked vegetables or diced fresh vegetables, you feel like. Serve and enjoy.

Bangers In Blankets

Bangers is English slang for pork sausages.

Serves 1–2

- **2–3 eggs**
- **Pinch baking soda (optional)**
- **Cooking spray or olive oil**
- **2–3 sausages or hot dogs**
- **Toothpicks (optional)**
- **Hot dog buns, toasted**

Prepare the omelette in the normal way, letting it get hardish all the way through. If it's thin enough, you won't need to flip it. Now slide it flat onto a plate.

Separately, fry one sausage per omelette. Alternatively, heat up a standard hot dog in the microwave, a frying pan, or some boiling water. Then, starting from one end of the omelette, roll the sausage up into the omelette. If you happen to have some toothpicks handy, fasten the far end of the omelette onto the sausage with a toothpick to stop it from unraveling.

If you still have time and inclination – and some hot dog buns around – toast half a bun lightly; hollow out the soft core of the bun leaving just the outer crust (your finger is the right tool for doing this); wedge the Bangers in Blankets into the scooped out hotdog bun.

Banana Omelette

This recipe pushes (but doesn't exceed) the seven minute barrier. But it's worth it. I'm afraid it also involves some butter which is generally not as healthy as olive oil.

But Daaa-ad...

Serves 1–2

1 banana
Brown sugar
Lemon juice
2 eggs
Pinch baking soda (optional)
Cooking spray or olive oil

Melt a pat of butter in your favorite frying pan. Cut one banana (for every two omelettes) in half lengthways. Fry the two halves until they are soft on the bottom; turn, cover with brown sugar, squeeze on lemon juice, and fry until they are soft on the top.

Once the banana halves are ready, start your omelette. Almost immediately tip one banana slice and half the juice onto the omelette (leaving the other half banana and juice for the next omelette). Finish the omelette. Garnish the top with a little more brown sugar and lemon juice. Serve as soon as possible since this dish tastes better hot and fresh.

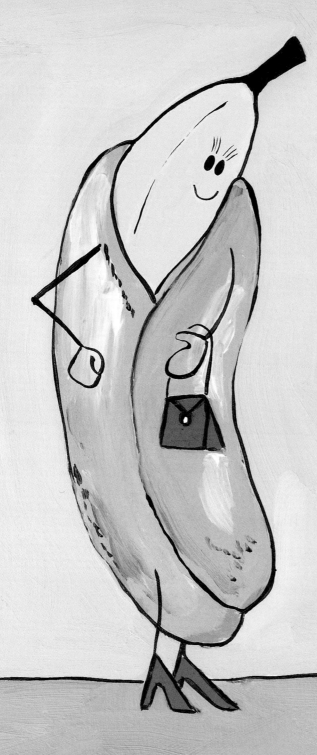

banana omelette

Jelly Omelette

This is a sweet omelette that, I guarantee, the kids will flip over. However, there is a right and a less right way to make it. The less right way is very good and very quick. It's certainly more than adequate for any kid under, say, 12. Even the most sophisticated of them don't really know batter from Batman. However, older kids (and you) may be able to tell the difference. The fact is that the right way is superb – although it does take a bit longer.

Serves 1–2

2 eggs
2 teaspoons sugar
Jam or marmalade

The less right way:

⟶ Crack two eggs per omelette into a bowl and mix with sugar. Then make the omelettes in the normal manner. As each omelette is setting up, add a good dollop of jam to its center, and then finish the job. If you like marmalade, you can also add some grated lemon peel to the mix, but that's a bit of a long run for a short slide. (One of my twins likes lemon curd, and Omelette au Richard Curd de Limon, a really bad pun on the French name of Robin Hood's royal liege, is his favorite.) When the omelette is complete, slide it onto a plate and add a dollop of jam, marmalade, or lemon curd, as the case may be, on top.

Serves 2–3

) **4 eggs**
) **¼ cup powdered sugar or sugar**
) **½ teaspoon vanilla**
/ **Jam**

The right way:

⟶ This makes two large or three medium-sized omelettes. Take four eggs and separate the whites from the yolks. In a small bowl, beat two of the yokes until they look whitish. Beat in sugar (powdered sugar is best, but ordinary white sugar will do) and vanilla. In a separate bowl, whip the four egg whites until they are pretty stiff. Now stir them lightly into the yoke mixture. (The blandness I complained about in the section here on how to make omelettes turns out to be an advantage when you are making sweet omelettes.)

When you've done all that, make the omelette in the ordinary way, add a dollop of jam inside, and another dollop on top, and Bob's your uncle.

CRÊPES

A more sophisticated version of omelettes is the famous French crêpe. (You will notice that crêpe has a circumflex accent over the "e" – that's the little hat. That's because it's missing an "s". Originally, it was spelled 'crespe,' or pretty similar to the English word 'crisp' which is interesting only because crêpes are not crisp.) If you'd like to try an alternative to omelettes, then give these crêpes a try.

Makes about 12 (9-inch) crêpes

> 1 cup all-purpose flour
> ½ cup milk (skim, 2%, or regular, as you prefer)
> 3 eggs
> ¼ teaspoon salt (if butter is salted, then omit salt)
> 2 tablespoons olive oil
> Filling (e.g., jam, marmalade, chocolate)

You make the crêpes by mixing all ingredients together except the oil. If you use a blender, you'll end up with a smooth paste. If you mix the batter by hand, you'll end up with some lumps in the paste. Squish the larger lumps with a spoon against the side of the bowl, but don't worry if smaller lumps remain, they'll disappear in the cooking process.

Use oil to grease the pan. Ladle one to two tablespoons of batter onto the middle of your frying pan. Tip the pan side to side until the crêpe is as thin as you can get it.

By the time you've done that (30 seconds or so), the crêpe will be ready to flip over. Brown it for no more than about 20 seconds on the other side, and remove quickly. Dump in the filling, and fold the crêpe over it.

Unlike thin, plain omelettes, your have to heat up the filling separately because the crêpe is so thin that, if you try to heat the filling while it's in the crêpe, you'll burn the crêpe to a cinder.

You can use the same fillings as used for an omelette in a crêpe, too. However, chocolate goes well with crêpes, but not with omelettes.

FRENCH TOAST

When you order French toast in a restaurant, it generally comes out dry. Chef Pierre Ange will share his secret so you can make it at home perfectly.

Serves 2–3

> 3 slices bread (preferably not fresh)
> 1 tablespoon sugar
> 1 cup milk
> 2 egg whites
> 1 egg yolk (optional)
> Olive oil for frying

Take some leftover bread, it can be fresh, but it's even better if it's on the stale side. If you bought a French baguette (you know, one of those long, thin loaves) and didn't finish it, by now it will be rock hard. If you can cut it at all, it will be perfect for French toast.

In a small bowl, dissolve sugar into milk. Pour the milk into a large flat pan. Then put in the slices of bread and soak them through with the milk. Spoon some milk over the bread to make sure it is completely soaked. When you've soaked up all the milk, decide if you have enough French toast. If not, prepare some more milk-soaked bread.

In a bowl, stir or beat the eggs just vigorously enough to liquefy them, as distinct from leaving gobs of individual whites. (There is no need to have any yolks in French toast. But you can add one whole egg to several whites if that makes you happy.)

Pour the whites over the soaked bread. Turn the bread over and pour over more egg whites. Cover the bread with as much egg as possible. Grease frying pan with olive oil and when pan is hot, fry first side of bread until golden brown. (A hot frying pan ensures that the toast will be crisper.) As you are frying, add more egg whites to the top of the soaked bread. Turn and complete frying.

What you will get is a crisp outer shell of egg whites and a deliciously soft, sweet inner core. No doubt, you will offer up a silent prayer of thanks to the Chef.

French French Toast
To go "over the top" with French toast, instead of bread use croissants, cake, or any other "farinaceous matter," as my dad used to call it, (made with flour) instead of bread. Oh my!

french toast

PANCAKES

Pancakes are incredibly easy to make...provided, of course, that you use a prepared pancake mix. Any brand will do. Follow the instructions on the pancake mix you prefer.

Of course, you could make your pancakes from scratch. However, they would probably be tougher and less tasty, and anyhow, why go to more trouble than you need to?

Since most mixes contain relatively little protein and are usually eaten with syrup, they have a lousy nutritional profile. Therefore, it's generally a good idea to add some egg whites (two or three for every cup of dry mix).

You can add almost anything to pancakes from sweet to savory foods. Here are a few unexpected variations with slightly different approaches and worth trying at home. For the rest, just make the pancakes according to the instructions, add some egg whites for protein, and either mix in our pour on top of the pancakes anything that comes to mind.

Pearcakes, Applecakes, and Other Fruit Pancakes

The key difference between the fruit-filled pancakes everyone serves (blueberry pancakes being a perennial favorite), and making the best fruit pancakes ever, is that the fruit take center stage. If you've got it, flaunt it.

Makes about 6 pancakes

> 6–12 slices fresh fruit (e.g., berries, bananas, pears, apples, or your favorite fruit)
> 1 egg
> Dash olive oil
> 1 cup pancake mix (prepackaged)
> 1 cup milk

Prepare the fruit by cutting into ¼-inch-thick slices and set aside. Mix all ingredients together. Pour batter into griddle or frying pan, forming approximately 2-inch diameter pancakes.

Take each slice of your fruit and press it into the top of the pancake so it covers at least half of the pancake's surface. If one slice isn't enough, use several pieces. As soon as the pancake starts to bubble, flip over to the other side, cooking each side for about 2 minutes. Serve fruit side up with your favorite topping.

When serving the pancakes, the fruit has warmed up, but not cooked. The fresh, uncooked fruit is much tastier than the cooked variety. I think you'll find this approach to making fruit pancakes is truly a cut above the rest!

Coke or 7-Up Pancakes

Actually, you can make this type of pancake with any soft drink. Sprite, Dr. Pepper, even ginger ale will do. They all taste pretty good.

Makes about 6 pancakes

> **1 egg**
> **Dash olive oil**
> **1 cup pancake mix (prepackaged)**
> **1–1½ cups Coke, 7-Up, ginger ale,**
>   **or other type of soda pop**

Mix egg and olive oil with pancake mix. Add Coke or other soda pop to combine the mixture into a viscous liquid.

In a griddle or frying pan, pour silver-dollar-size pancakes into pan, and wait for batter to bubble, then flip pancake to other side, cooking each side for about 2 minutes, or until desired doneness. Garnish with your favorite topping.

Coke pancake

Apple Flapjacks

Although, by and large, I prefer fruit pancakes (made the way the chef described in the recipe on page 59), Apple Flapjacks are the exception because the unique way the chef makes them imbues them with ultimate appleness.

Makes about 6 pancakes

> 1 egg white
> Dash olive oil
> 1 cup pancake mix (prepackaged)
> 1 cup applesauce
> A little water or apple juice

Mix together pancake mix, apple sauce, egg white and enough apple juice to make the batter the consistency of a viscous liquid. If the mixture is too thick, add a little more apple juice.

Pour the pancake mix into a griddle or frying pan, and wait for batter to bubble. Then flip pancake to other side, cooking each side for about 2 minutes, or until desired doneness. Garnish with applesauce and/or your favorite topping.

You may also want to top pancakes with fresh apples slices as describe on page 59. Go for it!

Death by Pancake

The Doubletree Hotel chain used to give its guests a gift of the most luxurious cookies. The cookies were replete, stuffed full of, overflowing with chocolate and nuts. They were irresistible.

You can achieve the same richness by adding handfuls of chocolate chips and nuts to your pancake batter. I like a mixture of slivered almonds and pecans best, but any nuts will do.

Makes about 6 pancakes

> 1 egg
> Dash olive oil
> 1 cup pancake mix (prepackaged)
> 1 cup milk
> ½ cup chocolate chips
> ½ cup chopped nuts

Mix all ingredients together. Pour batter into griddle or frying pan, forming nice, thick pancakes. As soon as the pancake starts to bubble, flip over to the other side, cooking each side for about 2 minutes. Garnish with your favorite topping.

Kartoffel Puffer

This is a German potato pancake. If you want to sound authentic, you'll obviously have to pronounce the words correctly. Your kids will be impressed. The first word, Kartoffel, is pronounced exactly as it is spelled. However, the "puff" in "puffer" is trickier. The German vowel sound is shorter than in the English word "roof" and longer than in "rough." The closest I can come is the vowel sound in "foot," or the sound you make when someone punches you in the stomach: "ouf."

Fortunately, the recipe is simpler than its pronunciation.

Serves 4–6

6 potatoes
1 egg white (per 1 cup potato mash)
Salt
1 tablespoon olive oil
Apple sauce or sugar for garnish

Grate up potatoes (or mash them up in a blender). The mash should not be too smooth; it should be a slurry of small strips of potato. Add one egg white to each cup of potato mash and sprinkle with a little salt.

In a frying pan, add olive oil and fry up each potato puffer, about the size of a silver dollar. It's time to turn them when the edge of the puffer becomes browned and starts to crisp.

Serve with apple sauce if you are a traditionalist. Otherwise, serve with sugar.

Grown-up Pancakes

One of the problems with most pancakes is that they are eaten with globs of syrup. This has the double disadvantage that it tends to kill the subtler tastes you have laboriously imparted to the stack (well, "laboriously" for a couple of minutes anyway); and that the syrup, to understate the case, is nutritionally challenged. Wouldn't it be nice, therefore, if you could make pancakes that don't require syrup, but that the kids would enjoy anyhow?

You can. And by calling them "grown-up," you'll probably turn them into a breakfast favorite.

Makes about 6 pancakes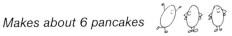

1 egg
Dash olive oil
1 cup pancake mix (prepackaged)
1 cup milk
½ cup bacon bits, cooked
American cheese slices

Mix together egg, olive oil, pancake mix, and milk. Add crisp bacon bits. (See page 20 for how to make bacon a relatively easy morning task.)

Now pour silver-dollar-size pancakes into a preheated frying pan, and brown lightly on one side. ("Lightly" is as soon as bubbles start to appear on the top of the pancake.) Immediately, flip the pancake and then completely cover the pancake with slices of American cheese. The pancake will be complete as soon as the cheese melts.

A small note of caution: don't pile these pancakes on top of one another because the cheese will stick and you'll end up with a big mess. However, if you have really hungry kids, you can layer a couple of pancakes on top of each other for a "Super Grown-up Pancake."

grown-up pancake

OATMEAL

Oatmeal is great, oatmeal is grand;
But ordinary oatmeal tastes rather bland.
Oatmeal is fiber, oatmeal is hot,
But nutritionally sound oatmeal is not.

Oatmeal contains no protein, almost no antioxidants, in fact almost nothing that is "good for you" except fiber. Empty calories; lots of empty calories, but very little nutrition.

On the other hand, an island of steaming hot oatmeal (called porridge in England) sprinkled with plenty of brown sugar, surrounded with a moat of milk, and maybe a pat of melting butter is nothing short of perfection, especially on a dull, cold, or rainy day. Cheers you right up!

Super Oatmeal

This is exactly the same as regular oatmeal in appearance, flavor, fiber content, and the serenity that comes from eating a good, solid, hot breakfast on a cold and miserable day. The difference is that Super Oatmeal is also nutritionally good for you. That is because …Ta-dah! … it's fortified by making it with milk that, like most milk these days, is vitamin enriched; and adding an egg white per serving of oatmeal.

By the way, even though you stir, the oatmeal it will probably stick to the bottom of the pan. It's just what oatmeal does. Oh well!

Serves 1–2

- **1 cup oatmeal**
- **½ cup milk**
- **1 egg white**
- **Brown sugar, milk, and butter**
  for topping (optional)

Add oatmeal, milk, and egg white to a saucepan and heat over medium-high heat. Stir constantly to avoid oatmeal sticking (excessively) to bottom of pan.

If you're in a hurry, you can also place all ingredients into a glass bowl and heat in the microwave for about 2–3 minutes, stirring halfway through cooking.

Top oatmeal with brown sugar, milk, and butter, if desired.

super oatmeal

Froatmeal

Serves 1–2

- **1 cup oatmeal**
- **½ cup milk**
- **¼ cup plain non-fat yogurt**
- **1 egg**
- **1 egg white**
- **¼ cup raisins**
- **1 cup diced fresh fruit (e.g., apples, apricots, bananas, blueberries, peaches, pears, plums, raspberries, strawberries)**
- **¼ cup chopped nuts (salted or honey roasted, if desired; optional)**
- **Salt**

In a saucepan over medium-high heat, combine oatmeal, milk, and yogurt.

Add whole egg, egg white, and raisins. Gradually bring the mixture to a boil, stirring as you proceed. Do this for 3–4 minutes until the oatmeal has the consistency of, well, oatmeal. (If it's a little on the thick side, add a splash more milk. You don't want it to be too thin because the juice from the fruit you'll be adding will thin it some.)

Add fruit. (Grapes, melon, and most citrus fruits are better savored cold.) Also, unless your kids have a peanut allergy or don't like nuts, add nuts to mixture. Stir just long enough for the fruit and nuts to heat up.

There you are: delicious, proteinaceous, fibrous, fresh, fruitious goodness!

Hoatcakes

Excellent though Froatmeal is, because it's pretty filling, it often happens that there is quite a lot of it leftover. You could, of course, serve it again the following day.

"Not again, Daaa-ad!"

Fortunately, you can offer a completely different meal with the leftovers. Heat a frying pan (hotter than normal), oil it up with olive oil, dump a tablespoonful of the Froatmeal (see recipe on page 68) into it, spread it out so that it is not too thick, and fry up a pancake (see recipe on page 58). If the pan is hot enough, you can crisp the hoatcake which makes it even better.

Serve with syrup as you would with any other pancakes, and you will have both elicited kudos and solved a leftover problem.

GRITS & CREAM OF WHEAT

Grits are an acquired taste. They are cornmeal powder that, when added to boiling water, turns into a bland, slightly gritty, slightly soupy paste. Unlike oatmeal which is normally eaten with sugar, grits usually have salt added and are eaten, in lieu of potatoes or rice, as a savory dish accompanying meals.

Even for breakfast, grits are often combined with fish or some other savory ingredient. For example, my mother-in-law enjoys grits mixed with sardines. I find this an unpleasant combination, but everyone has different tastes!

Some people dote on this regional dish, and I have to admit that they (the grits, I mean, not the people) are very versatile. Actually, in addition to using grits as a substitute for potatoes or rice in any "meat and potatoes" meal, for breakfast you can make anything with grits that you can make with oatmeal.

There is, however, one real saving grace for grits. It is that, when you make froatmeal with grits, it is legitimate (and you will amuse the children to no end) to call it …

Fritz

Grits (prepackaged)
½ cup sliced and diced fruit
   (per 1 cup grits)

Prepare grits following the instructions on the package. When the grits are nearly ready, add fruit to grits. (The package will tell you how many cups of grits you can expect to get from the amount of the powder/water you are cooking.)

The resulting Fritz is as good as anything you can make out of grits.

Cream of Wheat

Together with oatmeal and grits, this is the third of the triumvirate that, in themselves, are not particularly tasty or nutritious, but can be gussied up to be quite acceptable. This product (as the name indicates) is less gritty and creamier than grits. It is also sweet.

You can make almost anything with cream of wheat that you can make with oatmeal or grits. There are several favorite ingredients that taste great with cream of wheat.

Gourmet Cream of Wheat

This is standard cream of wheat with a good solid dose of cheese and bacon bits added.

Cream of wheat (prepackaged)
Cheddar cheese
Bacon bits (fried crisp)

Cook cream of wheat according to package instructions. Add cheese and crisp bacon bits to bubbling, slightly cooked cream of wheat. Stir to combine and serve.

Cream of Chocolate Wheat

This is cream of wheat with sliced almonds and chocolate chips. Some kids don't like nuts – so leave out the almonds. I prefer milk chocolate, but dark chocolate works fine, too.

> **Cream of wheat (prepackaged)**
> **Almonds, sliced**
> **Chocolate chips**

Cook cream of wheat according to package instructions. Add the sliced almonds as you are cooking the cream of wheat. Add the chocolate chips to fully cooked and gently bubbling cream of wheat in the saucepan. Stir as the chocolate melts, and you will have a light brown, chocolate flavored, delicious breakfast.

Alternatively, you can add them to an eating-size portion of very hot cream of wheat in a soup bowl. By stirring carefully, you can make an attractive chocolate swirl pattern in the bowl. Either way, this dish is a favorite with most kids.

OTHER DELICACIES

Count 'Em Fruit Salad

Fruit salad makes a nice breakfast change. As for Superola, add peanuts for protein. Serve it with Yogurt Crème (see page 75).

To make the dish fun, especially for younger kids, add small quantities of other nuts, raisins, any other dried fruit chopped fine, marshmallows (either miniatures or large ones cut into small pieces),

chocolate chips, or anything else that might blend in. Then tell your brood how many different ingredients there are, and challenge them to name all the ingredients.

Kids love this meal. The only problem is that, as they search for the ingredients, eating breakfast will take longer than normal!

Superola

Many families eat cereal for breakfast. They know it's not particularly good for them, but it's tasty, and it's certainly the path of least resistance. Indeed, we allow our kids to help themselves to a feast of an array of the stuff – sugaring, empty calorie, kid exploitation and all – when we want to sleep in on Sunday mornings.

However, there is one cereal that is reasonably nutritious and totally delicious. It is a form of granola that contains a pretty fair balance of protein, a little fat, some valuable fiber, fresh fruit vitamins, and of course, lots of carbohydrates.

The trick is to make a mixture of any cereals you happen to have in the house, and add peanuts for protein, and fresh fruit cut into pieces. (Any sort will do except citrus which will curdle the milk.)

Then, instead of regular milk, try Yogurt Crème.

Yogurt Crème

This is an excellent – and healthy – alternative to milk for use with cereal or any other food that requires added milk.

Take any non-fat fruit yogurt and thin it to the consistency of thick cream with milk, preferably 2% or skimmed, or even (horrors!) regular milk thinned with water.

Peach or Apricot Boats

Every now and then, thinking outside the box, Chef Pierre Ange creates something that, one might think, isn't breakfast at all...but works like breakfast. In the case of this recipe, assuming you have either peaches or apricots around (fresh or canned halves), the Chef has created the simplest breakfast of all.

Peaches or apricots (fresh or canned)
Cottage cheese or yogurt (any flavor)
Nuts
Raisins
Toast, slices

If using fresh fruit, cut the fruit in half and remove the pits. If using canned, then take out halved fruit. You now have little hollowed out canoes.

In a separate bowl, mix cottage cheese or yogurt with nuts and raisins. Fill the boats with cottage cheese or yogurt mixture. Serve the boats with slices of toast.

apricot boat

Index